A GUIDE TO GOATS
for beginners

Ashleigh Correll

Gauthier Publications
P.O. Box 806241
Saint Clair Shores, MI 48080
Attention Permissions Department

1st Edition
Gauthier Publications
www.EATaBOOK.com

ISBN: 9780692022627

TABLE OF CONTENTS

HISTORY

Goats are closely related to sheep and are one of the oldest domesticated species of animal that we know about. Neolithic (from about 10,200 BC – 2,000 BC) farmers originally began using goats as a source of meat and milk. However, they used practically every part of the animals, from their sinew, bones and hair, to their dung as fuel. Goat skin has also been used to make parchment, as well as used to make bottles to hold liquids during transport.

Their remains have been found at archaeological digs in western Asia which puts their time of domestication between 6000 and 7000 B.C.

Now, there are over 300 goat breeds across the world. And in 2011, the UN Food and Agriculture Organization stated that there were more than 924 million goats living around the world.

Goats have commonly been used as a source of hair, milk, meat and skins across the globe, and you may be surprised to find that this is still true today.

CARE & USES

In North America and Europe, certain breeds of goat are raised for meat, some are raised for milk, and some for fiber production to use for spinning and yarn. In dairy breeds, male goats that aren't used for breeding are generally slaughtered and used for meat, since they are unable to produce milk. In the meat breeds however, does and bucks are both used for meat. Certain breeds of goats used for fiber can also be used for meat, but they are generally only used for fiber as they can earn the breeder more over a lifetime of fiber production than if they were only producing meat once.

MEAT

Goat meat is said to taste similar to mutton (lamb meat) and some people say it also tastes similar to veal (calf meat.) One of the most well-known breeds of goat used for meat was introduced to the US in the 1990s, it is the South African Boer.

Generally, bucks over a year old are not used for meat. Since they are uncastrated, their meat isn't desirable for human consumption because it has a different taste and texture. Castrating male goats when they are young will keep this from happening.

Meat goats are usually kept in pastures year round, and do not need to be kept close to the barn since they aren't brought in unless they need special care, or if it is time for slaughter. They may get hay and supplements in addition to the pasture, but this is usually done more in the winter.

DAIRY

Goats actually account for about 2% of the world's milk supply each year. In their prime, a dairy goat can produce about 7 pounds (about 3 – 4 quarts) of milk per day. And since the cream of goat milk does not rise to the top like it does in cow milk, goat milk doesn't need to be homogenized.

Dairy goats are usually kept close to the place where they are milked, since they need to be milked every day. In addition to the grass they eat while pastured, their diet is usually supplemented with additional hay and sometimes supplements to help with milk production.

They will produce milk when they have a kid, or if they are continually milked they will also continue to produce milk. In Europe, they generally breed the does once or twice and then milk them for several years afterward without breeding them again. In the United States, they usually breed does every year to ensure continuing milk production. They usually spend their summers in pastures, and are sometimes kept in barns during the winter or during summer droughts.

OTHER USES

Goats have been used to clear land for hundreds of years. Since goats eat many kinds of plants that horses and other animals won't eat, they are very effective in clearing land. In the United States, some people have even started business where they rent their goat herds to people specifically to clear their land.

You may be surprised to find that goats' anatomy is similar to humans, and in some places they are used for medical training. In the US, goats started being used for this in the 1980s after they stopped using dogs for medical training.

It is also becoming increasingly more popular for people to keep goats as companion animals rather than for any sort of production or agriculture.

Some charities have started giving goats to poor people because they are cheaper and easier to maintain than other livestock.

SHOWING

Breed clubs, 4H Clubs, and FFA (Future Farmers of America) often hold shows for their members. Each animal is judged on things like conformation, breeding production, udder quality, and type specific things like muscle on meat types and fiber on fiber producing animals.

Goats that are registered with breed associations or who are the offspring of goats who have won awards and done well in the show arena are worth more, and are generally the most likely to be shown. In general, goats that are registered are worth more money because they can trace the animal's lineage, bloodlines and breeding information on the animal's sires and dams. This data can be very helpful in determining how successful an animal will be as a show animal, a dairy animal, or a breeding animal.

In organizations like 4H or FFA, shows also have showmanship classes. In these classes conformation of the goat is not judged, the pair is judged on the presentation and cleanliness of the goat and the person showing the goat. They are also judged on the exhibitor's skill in handling the goat as well. Basically, the goat isn't being judged, the handler is being judged on how well they prepared the goat and how well they handle it in the show pen.

COMMON GOAT BREEDS

BOER

The Boer goat gets it's name from the Dutch word "boer" which means farmer. It is thought that this name was chosen to distinguish this goat from the other kinds of goats being imported into South Africa.

This breed is primarily used for meat, and it is very popular in South Africa. It has been used with success in South Africa kept with cattle because goats are such good browsers and don't impact grass as much as cattle or sheep.

Boer goats have large horns, and long floppy ears. Bucks of this breed weigh between 250–300 pounds, and does weigh between 200–225 pounds. They also have an extended breeding season and are able to give birth 3 times every two years.

MYOTONIC

Myotonic goats are one of the few kinds of goats native to the U.S and they go by many names. They are also known as stiff legged goats, Tennessee Meat Goats, or the most popular name they are known by, Tennessee Fainting Goats. They are bred for meat, but are also gaining ground as pets.

When this breed of goat is scared or excited, it's muscles tense or lock up and they usually fall over and lay on the ground stiff for a few seconds. Basically, the chemicals that trigger the "fight or flight" response are not released

in Myotonic goats, which is why they "faint" instead of running or fighting.

There are several theories on how this goat came to exist, most involving either a mutation in a herd in Texas, or that they originate from a herd of goats brought from Nova Scotia.

Mytonic goats have been bred to be heavy, since they are used for meat production. They can be multi color, but are usually black and white. They are thought to be able to give birth twice per year, usually have an easy time giving birth, have good milk production and are known to be good mothers.

They also generally aren't very good climbers, so they can be slightly easier to keep contained than other breeds of goats.

NUBIAN

The Nubian goats are used for meat, dairy, and their hides. Since their breeding season is much longer than the average goat, they are able to produce milk year round.

Since this breed of goat is a milk producer and does well in hot climates, they have been used in other breeds to improve goats in other countries and allow them to better withstand the hot weather. This makes them better producers of meat and milk in hot climates.

Although the name Nubian comes from Nubia in Northeastern Africa , the term Nubian in the U.S. usually refers to the Anglo-Nubian which was made from breeding Nubians and British goats in the late 1800s.

Nubians are short haired, long legged, and have long ears. They are usually red, ran or black, but can be multicolored as well. Bucks usually weigh about 175, and does normally weigh about 135.

LAMANCHA

Lamancha goats originated in Oregon from the breeding of a type of short eared goat from Spain and LaMancha. They are hardy animals that are known for being able to withstand much hardship and still produce milk. They are primarily used as dairy goats.

This breed of goat exists in any color with a short shiny coat, but what they are really known for are their ears. Many people who do not have much knowledge about goats will think that there is something wrong with a LaMancha when they see it for the first time.

The ears can be "gopher ears" which are a maximum of one inch long, or may not even extend from the head at all and will have little cartilage or none at all. A goat with "elf ears" will have a maximum of 2 inches of ear. Either type of ear will be turned up or down at the end, and bucks can only be registered if they have a "gopher ear" type.

ANGORA

The mohair from an Angora goat dates back to biblical times and is referenced in the bible. The Angora goats came from the district of Angora in Asia, and their mohair became a valuable product in the 1800s.

Although France, Spain, and other European countries imported these animals in the 1800s, none of them led to much mohair production. In 1838 however, South Africa imported Angoras and they are now one of the third larges producer of mohair in the world. (Behind Turkey and the United States.)

The Angora goats are bred for their fine, smooth hair called mohair. Most Angoras in the United States yield about 5.3 pounds of mohair twice per year when they are sheared.

In this breed of goat, both does and bucks have horns. The buck's horns can reach two feet long, where the females generally don't grow longer than 10 inches. They also have long drooping ears, and are smaller than many kinds of goat. Mature bucks usually weigh 190–210 pounds and does weigh about 80–100 when full grown.

Angora goats do very well on pasture that even sheep would not do well on because they browse as high up on the bushes and trees as they can, but they are known to be more fragile than other breeds. If bad weather happens soon after a kid is born or soon after an adult is sheared, they may need some protection from the weather. They are also more susceptible to internal parasites like worms than sheep are.

Although Angoras are mainly used for their fiber, it is said that the meat tastes similar to mutton (lamb).

CASHMERE

Cashmere production is a fairly new business in the United States, with the first Cashmere goats being imported in the 1980s. These animals are favored because they are easy to take care of, do not jump like other breeds, and need little shelter because of the insulating properties of their fleece.

The fleece on a Cashmere goat is made of guard hairs and cashmere. The fleece is either separated and sold to spinners, or sold to wholesale buyers without separating. This breed is sheared once a year, and a mature buck can produce 2.5 pounds of fiber each shearing.

ANATOMY, HEALTH & CARE

Goats are smaller than most livestock like horses and cattle, but they are still larger than the smaller farm animals like chickens and turkeys. Depending on the breed and gender of the goat, they can range from 60 - 300 or more pounds per animal. Goats usually have a lifespan of 15 - 18 years, although things such as problems giving birth or a male being bred frequently can reduce their lifespan.

Goats use their horns for displays of dominance, protecting their territory and general defense of themselves or other goats. Contrary to popular belief, it is not only the male goats that have horns. Female goats often have horns, and this is a matter of breed and genetics, not gender.

Most goats have two horns, which can be different sizes or shapes depending on what breed or type the goat is. It is common among goats used in a commercial setting for the horns to be removed to prevent the goats from injuring other goats, humans or even themselves. If a goat gets stuck in a fence and tries to free itself, it can break its horn causing immense pain and blood loss.

When this happens, if the horn is not completely broken off, a veterinarian will sedate the goat, finish removing the horn, and then cauterize the wound to prevent further bleeding and infection. This is why many farms opt to have the horns re-

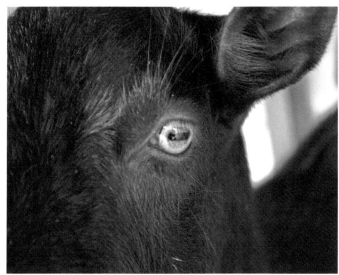

moved when the animal is young, to prevent problems like this.

One thing people are usually surprised to find out about goats, are that they have horizontal pupils. Their pupil runs horizontal and is narrow from top to bottom and long from side to side. Their irises are normally pale, which makes the pupil much easier to see than in other livestock. This design allows them to see 320 degrees around them with no blind spot in front of them like some other livestock have.

Depending on the breed, both male and female goats can have beards. Some breeds of goat also have wattles, which are small round pieces of flesh that hang down from the animal's neck. You have probably seen these on the bottom of a chicken's head, although they look much different on a goat.

Moving on to the body, goats have an udder with two teats, which differs from cattle that have four. Goats are also a ruminant, which means they have a stomach that is made up of four different chambers instead of one chamber like a human. Some other ruminants are cattle, llamas and deer.

BEHAVIOR

Goats are one of the most entertaining animals to watch, especially the kids. They are very intelligent and curious. Combine that with their ability to climb, fantastic balance, and great coordination, and you have a recipe for mischief.

Goats are avid climbers, jumpers, and enjoy attempting to escape from their enclosures. If the fencing keeping them in can be climbed, squeezed through, pushed over or spread apart,  they will most certainly figure out a way to escape. Once they have figured out how to escape, it's very likely they will do it again and that their fellow goats will learn from watching them and begin escaping as well.

Goats love to jump and climb on anything they have access to such as shelters, water tubs, stumps, rocks, and other goats, sheep, even horses that happen to be laying down. As long as the object or creature doesn't get up and walk away, the goat will have a grand old time jumping on or climbing it.

They are very curious and generally investigate any new surrounding or creature. Aside from smelling, they explore something new with their upper lip and their tongue. When they  are nibbling on something, they aren't always trying to eat it. Often they are just exploring it, although they are known for eating strange things.

In a herd, goats usually spread across their field and aren't as interested in staying close to each other as sheep would be. Even nursing kids and their

mothers will wander from each other a bit, instead of staying close to each other as a herd of sheep would. Male sheep are more likely than male sheep to charge at humans when they feel threatened, and generally turn and face a possible threat rather than run away

BREEDING

Goats reach the age when they will begin to breed at between 3 and 15 months. This can depend on the breed of goat and if they are fed a quality diet. In herds where many goats range the fields together, they may start breeding as soon as they reach maturity, but in operations where they are kept close to the barn and can be easily separated, many breeders like to wait to breed their does until they have reached 70% of her adult weight.

In temperate climates, breeding season starts as the length of the days grows shorter and ends in early spring. In areas nearer to the equator, goats can breed any time of the year. In those places, breeding de-pends more on the animals' diet than the time of year.

Female goats in any area come into heat every 21 days for anywhere from 2 hours to 2 days. Some signs a doe are in heat include her staying close to the buck, making more noise than normal, decreased appetite, and wagging her tail often.

Bucks go into rut the same time of year that does begin to go into heat. During this time, male goats often stay close to the does at all times, have a decrease in appetite, and will curl their lips often. Scent is also important in the breeding habits of goats. A male goat in rut has scent glands at the base of his horns, and the odor emanating from these helps make him attractive to the does. They often urinate on their beard and forelegs during this time as well.

Artificial insemination has also become popular in the goat industry, since it provides many different bloodlines and genetic backgrounds to be used, instead of limiting the breeder to the bucks they have on site.

Pregnancy in goats usually lasts from 148 – 152 days, with the doe usually giving birth to twins. Single kids and triplets are also common, and although less likely, quadruplets are possible as well.

When a doe give birth, it is referred to as kidding. Kidding usually happens fairly easily. The doe may seem worried, become restless, breathe heavy, and appear to have a sunken area ahead of her tail and hip. Once she has given birth, it is common for the doe to eat the placenta. This helps stop her bleeding, provides nutrients, and also reduces the scent of birth which can attract predators.

FEEDING

Although goats have a reputation for eating odd things, they do not actually eat aluminum cans and garbage.

However, where sheep and cows are grazing animals, goats are actually browsing animals. This combined with the fact that they are incredibly curious, they will taste and use their mouths to play with anything they think may be edible in order to decide if they are able to eat it or not.

Goats like to browse on shrubs and trees as well as plants. If you put a goat in a field with grass, plants, and trees. You will find the plants and trees lose their lower leaves as fast as the grass is eaten down.

Goats have a very wide diet of plants, and can even eat plants that are toxic to other animals.

 One of the reasons that goats are easier to maintain when kept in large fields, it that they will not eat food that has been soiled. This means a goat kept in a barn or small enclosure produces a lot of work for the owner in the area of cleaning the enclosure, wasted food, and replacing with clean food and water often.

Although goats are hardy animals, they enjoy eating plant leaves, so the owner must take care to ensure that none of the plants available to the animals are toxic. Hay should also be checked for mold before being given to the animals, as this can make them sick and even cause death in some cases.

A goat's adult size depends on the animal's diet while it is growing as well as the breed of the animal. Like any kind of livestock, the animal needs sufficient calories and protein while growing to make sure it reaches its full potential size wise. Generally, larger breeds of goats require more calories on a daily basis than smaller breeds of goats.

GOAT RELATED STORIES

In the Chinese zodiac, the goat is one of the animals in the 12 year cycle. Each animal relates to personalities and people born in a "year of the goat" are said to be creative, introverted, shy, and perfectionists.

Among the Greek gods, Pan had the upper body of a man, but the lower body and the horns of a goat. He was said to have created the pan flute, and most of the stories he is in portray him as chasing nymphs.

In Norse mythology, Thor is the god of thunder and his chariot is pulled by two goats. The myth goes that at night, Thor eats his goats and then wraps up their bones. Then in the morning, the goats come back to life and continue to pull his chariot. In one of the stories, Thor invites a farmer's son to eat with him. The boy broke one of the leg bones to suck the marrow from the bone, and the next morning the goat's leg was still broken when it came back to life. So Thor forced the boy to become his servant as punishment for the damage he had caused.

Northern European traditions around Christmas and Yule involve the "Yule Goat." Originally, a Yule Goat was a goat people slaughtered around yule, but it could also mean a goat that people had made out of straw.

In Gavle (a city in Sweden) there is a giant "Gavale Goat" made of straw erected every year. It takes two days to build the goat, and unfortunately it's often vandalized or set on fire.

Some mythological creatures are hybrids including parts of goats. In Greek mythology, the Chimera is a lion with the tail of a snake and a goat's head growing out of its back. Sa-

tyrs and fauns are part goat and part human, and the sign for Capricorn is a goat with a fish tail.

In the Bible, goats are mentioned many times. According to Jewish laws, a goat is considered a clean animal and could be slaughtered and eaten. A shofar is a horn used as a musical instrument in Jewish religious practices, and it is made of sheep or goat horns.

On Yom Kippur, a tradition was practiced in which two goats were chosen. One was allowed to escape into the wilderness, said to carry with it the since of the people, and the other goat was sacrificed. This practice is where the term scapegoat comes from.

GOAT RELATED TERMS

Banding—a form of castration using an elastic band to restrict blood flow.

Buck—a buck is an unaltered male goat, a male goat that has not been castrated.

Debudding or Disbudding—the process of removing a goat's horn "buds" so that the animal will not grow horns.

Doe—a doe is a female goat.

Heat—estrus, the time when a female goat is ready to reproduce.

Kid—a young goat that has not reached maturity, a baby goat.

Kidding—giving birth.

Mohair—the coat or fleece of an Angora goat.

Ruminant—a type of animal that chews cud, and has a 4 chambered stomach like goats and cows.

Rut—a time that coincides with a doe's heat, when a buck is ready to breed.

Wether—a wether is a male goat that has been castrated, wethers are not able to reproduce.

CPSIA information can be obtained
at www.ICGtesting.com
Printed in the USA
LVIC04n0252060515
437397LV00003B/5

* 9 7 8 0 6 9 2 0 2 2 6 2 7 *